CW00595137

Perth Walks

20 country walks within 30 minutes drive of the Fair City

Amenta Publishing

Copyright © 2004 Amenta Publishing

The right of James Carron to be identified as the Author of the Work has been asserted by him in accordance with the Copyright, Designs and Patents Act 1988.

First published in 2004
by AMENTA PUBLISHING

10 9 8 7 6 5 4 3 2 1

All rights reserved. No part of this publication may be reproduced, stored in a retrieval system, or transmitted without the prior written permission of the publisher, nor be otherwise circulated in any form of binding or cover other than that in which it is published and without a similar condition being imposed on the subsequent purchaser.

Cataloguing in Publication Data is available from the British Library.

ISBN 0-9547028-1-6

Typeset in Gill Sans MT by Amenta Publishing, Dundee.

Printed and bound in Great Britain by
Winters Pioneer Ltd, Dundee.

AMENTA PUBLISHING
Suite 68
17 Union Street
Dundee DD1 4BG

www.amentamedia.co.uk

Contents

Introduction   5

1. Kinnoull Hill   7
2. Deuchny Wood   9
3. North Inch   11
4. Buckie Braes   13
5. Mailer Hill   15
6. Craigie Hill   17
7. Quarrymill Woodland Park   19
8. Moncreiffe Hill   21
9. Pitmedden Forest   23
10. Portmoak Moss   25
11. The Tetley Trail   27
12. Bishop Hill   29
13. The Cleish Hills   31
14. Steele's Knowe   33
15. Glenearn Hills   35
16. Craig Rossie   37
17. Abernethy Glen   39
18. River Tay, Dunkeld   41
19. Birnam Hill   43
20. Mill Dam and Rotmell Wood   45
Useful contacts   47
Useful websites   47
Country Code   48

Introduction

Perth is an excellent base for walkers, located as it is within easy reach of upland areas such as Highland Perthshire, the Ochil Hills and the Lomond Hills.

However, closer to home there are some wonderful short walks. This book details 20 such routes, all within 30 minutes drive of the Fair City. They include woodland walks, lochside strolls and more strenuous hikes on to hill summits.

The routes range in length from just a mile to longer leg-stretchers and there's something for all ages and abilities. All promise pleasant countryside, fresh air and the chance to see a variety of flora and fauna in their natural habitat.

All of the walks in the book are accompanied by maps showing the route, text detailing it, and Fact Files. The Fact Files carry details of the start point, how to get there and the availability of parking. There is also useful information on the distance, the amount of time you should allow for the walk, the terrain you will encounter, any restrictions on dogs, and local facilities, including public toilets, picnic areas and friendly local pubs where you can enjoy coffee, a snack or a bar meal.

To enhance your enjoyment of the walks, the book also includes some handy tips on footwear, clothing, food and drink and recommended maps, plus some useful contact information.

Enjoy the walks!

Map legend

	Road		Cliffs/crags
	Track		Scree
	Path		Embankment
	Railway		Quarry
	Woodland		Stone wall
	Buildings		Loch/lochan/pond
	Hill summit		Bridge
	Communications/TV mast		

Maps

The best maps for following the routes in this book are the Ordnance Survey Explorer sheets. These offer a superb level of detail at a scale of 1:25,000. Sheets 366, 367, 369, 370 and 379 cover the walks in this book.

Footwear

Stout footwear is recommended for the majority of the walks in the book, although only a few require proper hillwalking boots. Sturdy boots or shoes with good gripping soles and ankle support are always a good idea when out walking, as is a decent pair of thick socks. Underfoot conditions may vary depending on the weather. A solid path can often become muddy after periods of rain.

Clothing

No special clothing is required for the low level walks. However, it is always a good idea to take a waterproof jacket, just in case the rain comes on. For upland routes pack additional warm clothing, such as a jersey or fleece, and a hat as it can often be cold or windy at higher levels.

Food and drink

All of the walks in this book can be completed in a morning or afternoon. Pack something to drink and some snacks, such as crisps, cereal bars or chocolate biscuits to keep you going.

Children

The majority of the routes in this book are suitable for families. The longer, upland ones, while too challenging for very young children, can be enjoyed by older children.

Dogs

Dogs can be taken on all of the routes in the book, although in some cases they will have to go on the lead, in part at least, due to livestock. Details of restrictions are given in each Fact File. When it comes to dog faeces, in parks or on pavements (where people walk or children play), it is always best to bag it and bin it. However, in open country encourage your dog to do its business away from paths and tracks and the faeces can be left to disintegrate harmlessly in the undergrowth. If your dog does crap on a path, follow the 'stick and flick' philosophy - pick up a stick and flick the faeces into the undergrowth where they can't be seen. Please don't bag them and then simply leave the bag on the ground.

Kinnoull Hill

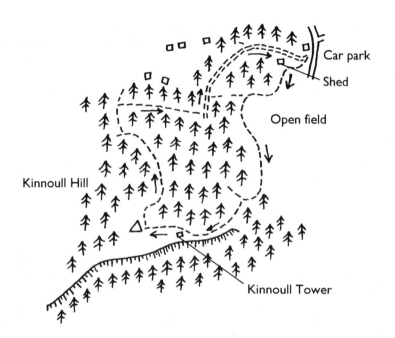

Fact File

Distance 3.2km/2 miles.

Time 1-2 hours.

Map OS Landranger 58; OS Explorer 369.

Start Forestry Commission Jubilee car park, grid ref NO 145236.

Parking Large free public car park.

How to get there Follow the road out of Perth from the north end of Perth Bridge, up past Murray Royal Hospital and continue out into open countryside to reach the car park, 3km from the bridge.

Terrain Well-defined tracks and paths through woodland.

Dogs No restrictions.

Facilities None on the route but plenty of choice in Perth, a short drive away.

The tower on Kinnoull Hill is one of Perthshire's best known landmarks, standing proud atop steep cliffs above the River Tay. Thankfully these plunging crags don't have to be negotiated to reach this prominent folly; there's a well-graded woodland path.

Leave the Forestry Commission's Jubilee **car park** by a path at its southern end, leading to the public road. Cross and, on the other side, follow a path up to a wooden gate. Go through and the route heads to the left of a wooden Forestry Commission **shed** to join up with the edge of an **open field**. It skirts along above the field, curving left and then right to reach a junction. Go left here and the path continues to run along the edge of the field for a short way, before rising into tall broadleaved woodland. The route climbs beneath the trees, curving right higher up to reach a junction.

Go left here and the route rises on to the top of steep cliffs that plunge down into the Tay valley below. Signs warn of the potential danger here but as long as you stick to the path you'll be fine. The gentle ascent soon ends as you emerge from the trees at **Kinnoull Tower**, an 18th century folly constructed by the 9th Earl of Kinnoull and modelled on the castles of the Rhine valley in Germany. There are magnificent views from this elevated spot across the River Tay to Fife.

Stay on the main path, following it down into a leafy cleft in the hillside. The way curves left, rising on to the summit of **Kinnoull Hill** where again there are dangerous cliffs to be aware of. Close to the top is a stone table built by the earl as a picnic spot. It's interesting to note that around 70 years ago, Kinnoull Hill was practically bare of trees. Since then, commercial planting and natural regeneration have remedied that and there is now almost complete tree cover and, with it, a diverse range of animals and birds, including red squirrels, wood mice, sparrowhawks, crossbills, coal tits and jays.

To begin the descent, head north on a track leading down to a junction. Go right here to pick up a path which drops through mixed woodland. Further down, another junction is reached. Bear right here and at the next junction, a short way on, go right again and a path heads east through the trees to join a track.

Turn left and the way heads north. Ignore a track on the right a little way on and continue as the route curves right. Stay with the main track at the next junction and it leads you back to the start, emerging on to the public road just beyond the wooden Forestry Commission **shed**.

Deuchny Wood

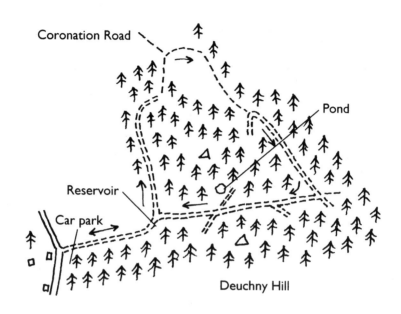

Fact File

Distance 3.2km/2 miles.

Time 1-2 hours.

Map OS Landranger 58; OS Explorer 369.

Start Forestry Commission Jubilee car park, grid ref NO 145236.

Parking Large free public car park at the start.

How to get there Follow the road out of Perth from the north end of Perth Bridge, up past Murray Royal Hospital and continue out into open countryside to reach the car park, 3km from the bridge.

Terrain Well-defined tracks and path through woodland.

Dogs No restrictions.

Facilities None on the route but plenty of choice in Perth, a short drive away.

Deuchny Wood is a commercial forestry plantation on the outskirts of Perth. It is home to a network of tracks and paths, including the ancient Coronation Road, used by Scotland's kings and queens in days gone by.

Leave the Forestry Commission's Jubilee **car park** at its north end, turn right and follow a steep track up to a gate and **reservoir**. Turn left here and the track flattens out to contour round the hillside, engulfed completely in a woodland of tall Scots Pine trees. The way curves right and, a short way after the bend, a path branches left. Follow this down to cross a fence and join **Coronation Road**, an historic right of way used by the kings and queens of Scotland as they travelled between Scotland's ancient capital of Scone, where the nation's monarch was traditionally crowned, and Falkland Palace, in Fife.

Turn right and the track, often used by pony trekkers, leaves the woodland and heads out over an open field, bearing right to meet the Langley Burn. Underfoot conditions can be muddy here as you follow the burn upstream through a sheltered valley flanked by ash and oak trees.

A gate leads back into the Forestry Commission plantation and, carrying straight on through the base of the glen, a good track makes for easy walking in a wide break in the trees and a T-junction is soon reached.

Turn right here and a good forest track climbs round the northern flank of **Deuchny Hill**, the site of an ancient hill fort occupied around 2000 years ago. Carry straight on at the next junction and the route passes a disused curling **pond**. This had silted up and become overgrown with rushes and grass. However, in 1991 the pond was dug out in a bid to attract aquatic life to the area.

From here, follow the track straight downhill, ignoring tracks on the left and right, to reach the Jubilee car park and the end of the walk.

North Inch

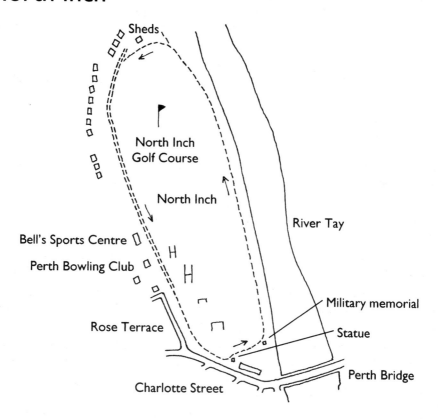

Fact File

Distance 2.4km/1.5 miles.

Time 1 hour.

Map OS Landranger 53; OS Explorer 369.

Start Rose Terrace, Perth, grid ref NO 117240.

Parking On-street parking in Rose Terrace costs 50p for one hour.

How to get there From the centre of Perth, follow Kinnoull Street north and turn right into Atholl Street. Rose Terrace is the next street on the left.

Terrain Surfaced path and track throughout.

Dogs No restrictions.

Facilities Café and restaurant at Bell's Sports Centre.

The centre of Perth is sandwiched between two parks – the North Inch and the South Inch. Both are pleasant open spaces offering an escape from the hustle and bustle of urban life. The Inches were gifted to the city by King Robert III in 1377 and over the years local people have made good use of them, grazing their animals or enjoying sporting pursuits.

The North Inch incorporates rugby and football pitches, a cricket field and golf course. In the 17th century there was a horse racing circuit here and this walk follows pretty closely the route taken by those early jockeys.

Enter the park from **Rose Terrace**, which has some fine Georgian architecture, and, when you join the main path, turn right. The route curves round the southern end of the **North Inch** to reach a rather eroded **statue** of Prince Albert. Bear left here and follow a paved walkway through stone gateposts to an imposing **military memorial** dedicated to the 42nd/73rd Highland Regiments of the Black Watch.

A surfaced path heads north from here, running along above the **River Tay**. There are plenty of benches, should you fancy stopping to enjoy the view across the water or feed the ducks.

Further on the path enters the **North Inch Golf Course** and, although none of the fairways cross the route, walkers are advised to watch out for any stray balls.

The path reaches a junction. Turn left and follow it through a gap in a stone wall. The route curves left, passing golf course **sheds** to join a wider, tree-lined avenue. This heads south below houses, the golf course to the left.

Beyond the fairways are football and rugby pitches and, in due course, the walk passes the **Bell's Sports Centre**. A short signed detour at this point will take you to the Black Watch Museum which charts two and a half centuries of military history of the 42nd/73rd Highland Regiments and is well worth a visit.

Carry straight on along the track, passing **Perth Bowling Club**, to finish the walk.

Buckie Braes

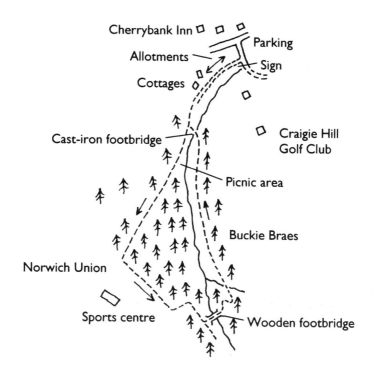

Cherrybank Inn

Parking

Allotments

Sign

Cottages

Cast-iron footbridge

Craigie Hill
Golf Club

Picnic area

Buckie Braes

Norwich Union

Sports centre

Wooden footbridge

Fact File

Distance 1.2km/0.75 mile.

Time Under 1 hour.

Map OS Landranger 58; OS Explorer 369.

Start Junction of minor road leading up to Craigie Hill Golf Club, behind Cherrybank Inn, grid ref NO 101225.

Parking Roadside parking at the start.

How to get there Follow Glasgow Road from the centre of Perth and turn left at mini roundabout on to B9112, signed for Cherrybank Gardens. Take the first road on the left, signed for Craigie Hill Golf Club, and then turn right at next junction.

Terrain Well-defined path through woodland.

Dogs No restrictions.

Facilities None on the route but the Cherrybank Inn near the start point offers snacks and bar meals.

Buckie Braes is a leafy wooded glade on the southern edge of Perth. Small streams meander down through the trees and there's a very pleasant picnic area in the base of the glen. A circular path offers a short but enjoyable country walk.

A green sign for **Buckie Braes** Adventure Play Area and Woodland Walk marks the start of the route. Go right here, following a track up past **allotments** on the right to a pair of **cottages**. Walk past the cottages and, at the end of the track, a path continues to a **cast-iron footbridge**. Don't cross but continue straight on, an obvious path following a fence uphill.

The way passes through mixed woodland of oak, ash, beech, holly and silver birch, rising above a grassy **picnic area** down to the left. To the right, beyond the fence, are the well tended grounds of insurance company **Norwich Union's** Perth offices.

The ascent is relatively short, but quite strenuous. Further up, the path turns left, skirting above the top of the den and below a **sports centre** and bowling green linked to the insurance company.

A short way on, it curves left and then right to reach a **wooden footbridge** spanning a stream. Cross and, a few metres on, wooden steps descend to cross another burn lower down.

The path descends more steps further down. Ignore a pair of wooden bridges on the left and continue along the main path to reach the **cast-iron footbridge**. Cross, turn right and retrace your steps back to the start.

Mailer Hill

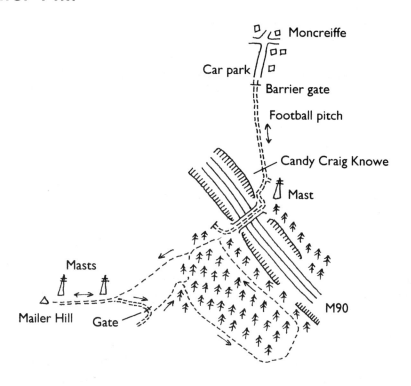

Fact File

Distance 3.6km/2.3 miles.

Time I hour.

Map OS Landranger 58; OS Explorer 369.

Start Craigie Hill Community Woodland car park, grid ref NO 108217.

Parking Large free car park.

How to get there Follow Edinburgh Road from centre of Perth, turn right on Gleneagles Road, signed for Community Woodland. Car park is at the top and is well signed.

Terrain Well-defined tracks and paths throughout.

Dogs Sheep grazing on Mailer Hill where dogs will need to be on the lead.

Facilities None on the route, but plenty of choice in Perth.

Mailer Hill is a low peak to the south of Perth, The walk begins at a public car park in the **Moncreiffe** area of the Fair City and climbs through pleasant mixed woodland and over open grassland to the summit where there are fine views across the River Earn valley.

At the top of the **car park** there's a black **barrier gate**. Walk round this and follow a good track south, up past a **football pitch** enclosed by a high fence. The way continues to rise gently, skirting the edge of open parkland sloping away to the left. Higher up the track curves right, round **Candy Craig Knowe**, to reach a junction.

Carry straight on, ignoring the track on the left that leads up to an aerial **mast**. The way skirts through scrub woodland before curving left to a bridge over the **M90** motorway.

Cross and, once over, the track curves right to reach a gate leading into a field. Just before this go left on a path which enters woodland. A short walk into the trees leads to a junction at a broken-down wall. Carry straight on here along a good path which runs close to the edge of the plantation, rising through oak, beech and silver birch trees.

Continue up to a post and wire fence with a wooden stile. Cross this and head over open grass to reach a pair of **masts** on **Mailer Hill**. Join a grassy track next to the compound and follow this west to a second pair of masts. Beyond these a trig-point on the summit of Mailer Hill is reached.

Head back to the first compound then follow the track down to a locked **gate**. Cross this (there's a gap in the adjacent fence for dogs) and turn left, an obvious path passing a broken gate and running beneath overhead power lines. It heads through gorse then curves right, entering woodland at a broken-down wall.

Back in the trees, bear right and an obvious path heads south-east, following the edge of the plantation. It descends to the southern tip of the woodland where it curves left at a makeshift wooden bench. The path continues along the edge of the woodland, crossing a muddy burn before climbing to reach the broken-down wall encountered earlier in the walk.

Turn right to return to the bridge spanning the **M90** motorway and retrace steps from here to the start.

Craigie Hill

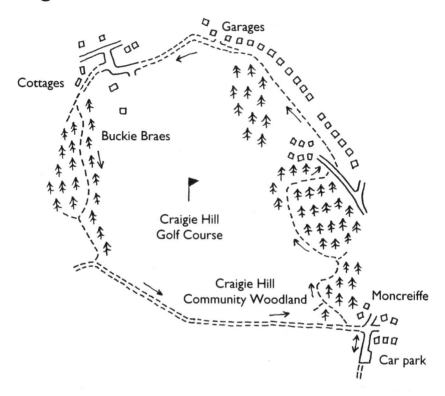

Fact File

Distance 3.2km/2 miles.

Time I hour.

Map OS Landranger 58; OS Explorer 369.

Start Craigie Hill community woodland car park, grid ref NO 108217.

Parking Large free car park at start.

How to get there Follow Edinburgh Road from centre of Perth, turn right on Gleneagles Road, signed for Community Woodland. Car park is at the top and is well signed.

Terrain Well-defined tracks and paths throughout.

Dogs No restrictions.

Facilities None on the route, but plenty of choice in Perth.

This walk round Craigie Hill begins in the **Moncreiffe** area of Perth, on the southern edge of the Fair City. Leave the car park and head down to the road junction below. Turn left here, passing round a metal gate a few metres on. Bear left and enter **Craigie Hill Community Woodland** at a wooden gate.

A wide grassy path rises gently from the gate before levelling off. At a junction a short way on carry straight ahead and soon the track curves right, descending quite steeply to another junction. Bear left here and the way rises past a picnic table.

Continue to another junction and go right. The track descends, passing above new housing to the left, to reach a wooden kissing gate. Go through and a short path leads down to a public road.

Turn right and follow the road for a short distance until you reach the start of a surfaced path on the left. This runs along the back of gardens to reach a junction. Go straight on here, the way skirting between local authority houses to the right and **Craigie Hill Golf Course**, up to the left. It passes behind **garages** and continues along above a wooded den and stream to reach a junction below the entrance to Craigie Hill Golf Course.

Bear right and follow the road as it curves down to a junction where there's a green sign for **Buckie Braes** Adventure Play Area and Woodland Walk. Go left here, following a track up past allotments on the right to a pair of **cottages**. Walk past the cottages and, at the end of the track, a path continues to a cast-iron footbridge.

Cross the bridge and a wide path rises through mixed woodland, a small stream and picnic area to the right. Stay on the main path, ignoring a number of smaller paths branching left and right.

Higher up, climb wooden steps to reach a wooden footbridge. Cross and turn left. A sheltered path follows a green chainlink fence. A short way on it curves right and then left, crossing a stream to emerge on to a track.

The track on the right leads to a bridge under the M90. Don't take this but carry straight on, the route skirting along the edge of the golf course, an open field to the right. Continue through a wooden gate and follow the track back to the start.

Quarrymill Woodland Park

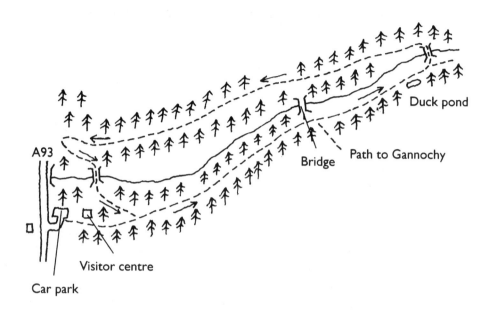

A93

Duck pond

Bridge   Path to Gannochy

Visitor centre

Car park

Fact File

Distance 1.5km/1 mile.

Time Under 1 hour.

Map OS Landranger 53; OS Explorer 369.

Start Quarrymill Woodland Park visitor centre, grid ref NO 119252.

Parking Free car park. This opens at 8am and closes at 4pm in the winter and 7pm in the summer.

How to get there From Perth Bridge follow the A93 Perth to Blairgowrie road north for 1.3km and Quarrymill Woodland Park is on the right.

Terrain Well-graded paths throughout.

Dogs Dog owners are requested to keep their pets on the lead throughout.

Facilities A coffee shop run by Macmillan Cancer Relief at the visitor centre is open daily except Sundays from Easter to late autumn. There are public toilets at the visitor centre.

Quarrymill Woodland Park, near Scone, offers walkers three very pleasant way-marked trails. The two shorter ones are accessible to wheelchair users while the longer Pine Tree Walk, featured here, rises from the base of the leafy den to meander through tall stands of Scots Pine, with elevated views over the woodland park.

Until around 150 years ago this tranquil spot was a hive of industry. Stone was quarried here for building and mills were constructed along the stream to grind bone meal, spin cotton and extract starch from potatoes. The park is now owned by the Gannochy Trust.

Leave the **car park** and head right, round the **visitor centre**. A good path strikes north, following the lively burn upstream. It passes through grassy parkland dotted with trees before the way narrows, the path skirting below steep slopes of broken rock to reach a substantial **bridge**. Don't cross but carry straight on to reach a junction with wooden steps climbing to the right. This is the start of a **path to Gannochy**.

Again, carry straight on to reach a **duck pond**. The way crosses the outflow, but there's a short detour on the right, leading to a wooden platform above the water. Back on the main path, continue east to reach a bridge over the burn. Cross and the path bears left, heading west back down the den.

It gains height by way of a flight of wooden steps leading to a junction of paths higher up. Go right here, climbing another set of steps. The path runs level through Scots Pine trees to reach a viewpoint with wooden seats.

There's another viewpoint a little further on and, beyond this, the path descends through rhododendron bushes towards the **A93** road. At the bottom of wooden steps, the way curves left and heads over open grass to a wooden footbridge. Cross and a path leads up to the visitor centre.

Moncreiffe Hill

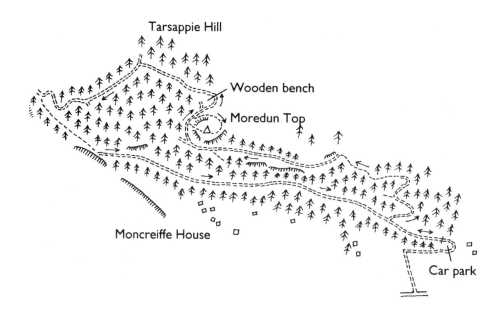

Tarsappie Hill

Wooden bench

Moredun Top

Moncreiffe House

Car park

Fact File

Distance 8km/5 miles.

Time 2-3 hours.

Map OS Landranger 58; OS Explorer 369.

Start Woodland Trust Moncreiffe Hill car park, grid ref NO 154193.

Parking Free car park.

How to get there Follow the A912 south from Perth towards Bridge of Earn. Just before the road crosses the River Earn, go left on road signed for Rhynd and Elcho Castle. The third track on the left, 2km from the junction, is signed for Moncreiffe Hill. Follow this to the car park.

Terrain Well-defined tracks and paths through woodland with some strenuous ascent early on in the route.

Dogs No restrictions.

Facilities None on the walk, but Bridge of Earn has shops and pubs, serving bar meals.

Moncreiffe Hill is a familiar landmark to anyone travelling to Perth on the M90. The motorway nudges the craggy slopes but within the tranquil wooded enclave you could be a million miles from the hustle and bustle of the heavy traffic so close at hand.

Walkers are welcome to explore the 333 acres of mixed broadleaf and conifer forest on the south side of the hill which was bought by the Woodland Trust in 1988. Keep your eyes peeled and you may spot red squirrels, green woodpeckers, roe deer and buzzards.

Pass through a wooden gate at the top of the **car park** and a wide path climbs steadily through the trees to a junction. Turn right here and the route continues to climb, more steeply now, curving right and then left to a junction where a grassy track heads west. Don't take this but bear right, staying with the main track as it rises through a mix of conifers, oak and sycamore, the grassy forest floor dotted with pink foxgloves.

The track curves left as it gains height and the gradient eases off to run fairly level through Scots Pine, emerging at a viewpoint. Rest for a moment in the purple heather and enjoy vistas south over the River Earn to the Ochil Hills.

The path disappears into the trees again, descending slightly before widening into a track. This runs level, passing through Scots Pine and larch woodland, before descending gently. Ignore a track branching off on the left and, do likewise a little further on when another track joins from the left. Beyond this the way reaches a junction.

Go right on a grassy path which climbs to a junction below the summit. Bear right here on a grassy path which curves round the northern slope of **Moredun Top**, rising on an even gradient to the summit cairn. The site of an ancient fort, Moredun Top offers panoramas north to Perth and east over the River Tay and Carse of Gowrie.

Return to the junction below the summit, turn right and a short walk on there's another junction. Go right here and the way leads to a **wooden bench**. Continue on and the track curves left, descending into more densely packed conifers. Lower down it passes between high fences to reach a junction above open fields.

Go left and follow this track as it rises gently to reach another junction. Bear right here and a pleasant grassy track drops through larch, skirting the edge of an open field further on. It curves to the left to reach its terminus above a wooden gate. Carry straight on along a narrow path. This links up with a track just above the motorway. Turn left and head east along the track. It climbs gently through mixed woodland, eventually reaching the junction of tracks above the car park. Retrace your steps from here to finish the walk.

Pitmedden Forest

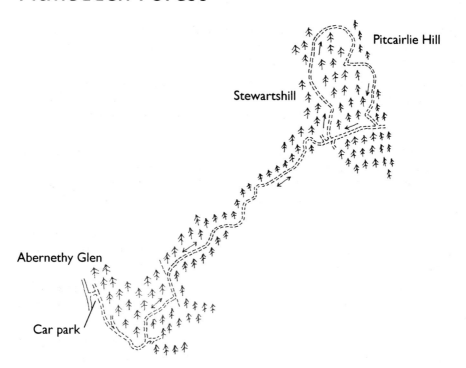

Pitcairlie Hill

Stewartshill

Abernethy Glen

Car park

Fact File

Distance 12km/7.5 miles.

Time 2-3 hours.

Map OS Landranger 58; OS Explorer 370.

Start Pitmedden Forest car park, Abernethy Glen, grid ref NO 188141.

Parking Small free car park.

How to get there Follow M90 south to junction 9, Bridge of Earn. Join A912 and follow it south-east to roundabout at Aberargie. Go left on A913 and, 1.5km on, turn right and follow minor road signed for Glenfoot and Strathmiglo up through Glenfoot into Abernethy Glen. Car park is 2.5km on from A913 junction, on left.

Terrain Easy to follow forest tracks. Keep an eye out for mountain bikes and occasional vehicles on the tracks. Route is suitable for mountain bikes throughout.

Dogs No restrictions.

Facilities None.

Straddling the border between Perthshire and the Kingdom of Fife, Pitmedden Forest was once the playground of the royals. From Falkland Palace, the kings and queens of Scotland rode out here in pursuit of wild boar. The original forest was largely felled to provide wood during the First World War, but it was later replanted by the Forestry Commission with Scots Pine, Sitka and Norway spruce and remains a commercial plantation under their control.

From the **car park**, the track rises south, running parallel with the public road through **Abernethy Glen** for a short distance before it curves left to reach a junction. Ignore the route on the left and continue along the main track, which goes on climbing, curving left to reach another junction a short way on.

Go left here, the track rising gently through tall stands of predominantly Scots Pine trees, curving right and then left. There's a clearing a short way on and another junction where a grassy track strikes off to the left. However, stay with the main track as it heads back into the trees, descending slightly before it starts to rise once again.

Further on, the route twists and turns a couple of times to reach the edge of the forest where views open out south to the Lomond Hills, the prominent rounded summits of East Lomond and West Lomond easily recognisable.

The track skirts the edge of the plantation, bordering land invaded by spiky gorse bushes. Fields slope into the valley below and views stretch out across the fertile Howe of Fife.

The way curves past an open area of ground, descending to another junction. Ignore the track on the left, which leads to the farm at **Stewartshill**, and carry straight on, round a barrier gate, to a crossroads. Turn left and follow the track north. Initially the route is hemmed in by tall trees. But these soon disappear to offer fine views over the Tay and Earn valleys, the two rivers flowing through farmland to meet just west of Mugdrum Island. You may be lucky enough to spot buzzards here, catching air currents high above the plantation. They feed on the healthy population of rabbits living in the woods and surrounding fields.

The track is lined with wild raspberry plants and blaeberry bushes, providing a refreshing snack for walkers towards the end of July and during early August when the fruit is ripe for picking.

Curving right, the way climbs under electricity pylon lines before turning east and then south, heading back under the wires. It rises around the northern flank of **Pitcairlie Hill**, passing below the line on two further occasions, then heads south to reach a junction. Turn right here and the track descends to the crossroads reached earlier in the walk. From here, retrace your steps back down the forest track to the car park.

Portmoak Moss

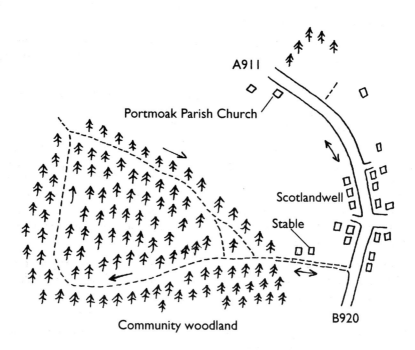

A911

Portmoak Parish Church

Scotlandwell

Stable

B920

Community woodland

Fact File

Distance 3.4km/2 miles.

Time 1 hour.

Map OS Landranger 58; OS Explorer 370.

Start Portmoak Parish Church, by Scotlandwell, grid ref NO 183019.

Parking Large free car park adjacent to church. This is available for public use except on Sundays before 11.30am when it is used by churchgoers.

How to get there Follow the M90 to junction 7, Milnathort, and then the A911 to Scotlandwell. Portmoak Parish Church is on the right, just before Scotlandwell is reached.

Terrain A low-level route with well-defined paths through woodland.

Dogs No restrictions.

Facilities The Well Country Inn, Scotlandwell, serves morning coffee, snacks and bar meals.

Portmoak Moss is a small community woodland located on flat land just east of Loch Leven. At the heart of the plantation is a raised peat bank. This elevated piece of ground was formed after the last ice age when the area flooded. Over the years changing water levels and temperatures resulted in the formation of peat as the vegetation rotted in water-logged soils.

For many years this natural resource provided fuel for locals and also turf for roofing. However, in the early 1960s the area was drained and planted with mixed conifers, spruce pine and larch.

Now in the care of the Woodland Trust and the local community, efforts have been made to encourage the return of native species such as Scots Pine, birch, rowan and willow, setting the scene for a pleasant short walk.

Leave the car park at **Portmoak Parish Church**, cross the public road and turn right. A pavement, narrow in places, leads into **Scotlandwell**. Carry straight on at the road junction in the heart of the village, following the **B920**. As you leave Scotlandwell, turn right on to a track signed for Portmoak Moss and Kinness Wood. This passes a **stable** and wastewater pumping station, both on the right, to reach a gate at the entrance to the **community woodland**. Beyond this there's an interpretation board and, a little further on, carved wooden benches.

Carry straight on along the path, ignoring a couple of paths coming in from the right. The way runs west through pleasant, well-established woodland and, in due course, reaches a set of steps rising on to the peat bank.

As you go you may be lucky enough to spot some of the wildlife that lives within the trees. There are 22 species of bird here, including the woodpecker, long-eared owl and buzzard, plus animals such as roe deer and red squirrel.

Further on, the path curves right and, as you head north now, another set of steps descends the peat bank. Further on, the way emerges from the trees at the northern tip of the plantation.

Bear right here. The path skirts along the northern edge of the wood, although remains firmly within the trees. It rises on to the peat bank once more further on at a set of steps.

There's a junction some way on; carry straight on here to join the path taken earlier in the day. Turn left to return to the gate at the entrance of the woodland. Retrace your steps from here back to the start.

The Tetley Trail

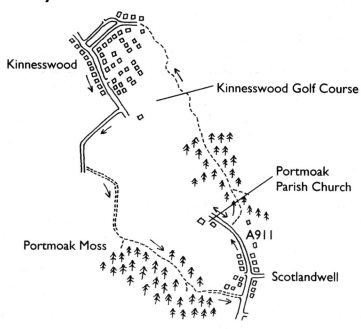

Kinnesswood

Kinnesswood Golf Course

Portmoak
Parish Church

A911

Portmoak Moss

Scotlandwell

Fact File

Distance 5km/3 miles.

Time 1-2 hours.

Map OS Landranger 58; OS Explorer 370.

Start Portmoak Parish Church, by Scotlandwell, grid ref NO 183019.

Parking Large free car park adjacent to church. This is available for public use except on Sundays before 11.30am when it is used by churchgoers.

How to get there Follow the M90 to junction 7, Milnathort, and then the A911 to Scotlandwell. Portmoak Parish Church is on the right, just before Scotlandwell is reached.

Terrain A low-level route with well-defined tracks and paths throughout.

Dogs There is sheep grazing on the hillside above Kinnesswood Golf Course where dogs will need to be on the lead.

Facilities There is a shop in Kinnesswood and two pubs on the route, the Lomond Country Inn, Kinnesswood, and the Well Country Inn, Scotlandwell, both of which do morning coffee, snacks and bar meals.

The Tetley Trail is a well established waymarked trail created by the local community and supported by the tea company, characters from their popular animated TV adverts appearing on information boards and markers.

Leave the car park, cross the road and turn right, following the pavement towards **Scotlandwell**. Just beyond the Scotlandwell road sign, turn left on a path signed for Bishop Hill. The way climbs wooden steps and continues up to a stile. Cross and walk up the edge of a grassy field to another stile where there's a Woodland Trust sign for Kilmagad Hill.

Once over the stile, turn left and a good path follows a fence along the lower edge of predominantly oak woodland with views west to Loch Leven. The way rises gently to a junction of paths and waymarker. Go left here and the path skirt along the side of the hill, through mixed broadleaves before descending to a recently planted area of saplings.

Stay with the path to reach a stone wall and kissing gate on the northern edge of the plantation. The route leaves the woodland here and heads across bracken-covered hillside, skirting above **Kinnesswood Golf Course**. The route rises and falls as it negotiates a series of gullies to reach another wooden kissing gate. Don't go through this, but continue straight on, following the fence. The path curves left and then right and, further on, passes a wooden bench, a fine place to stop for a breather and admire an uninterrupted view over Loch Leven. This seat has been dedicated to the actor Brian Glover, the voice of the Gaffer character in the Tetley Tea TV adverts, who died in 1997.

The path crosses a stream further on and passes above a fenced enclosure. Continue straight on and the way curves left, descending to a gate. Beyond this a short section of path meets up with a surfaced road. Follow this down through the houses of **Kinnesswood**. Where the road forks, take the left arm and continue down to the main street. Turn left and follow this south, passing a shop and Post Office, a filling station opposite, and then the Lomond Country Inn. Continue on and beyond 40mph signs, cross the road and turn right down a surfaced road signed for Portmoak Moss and Scotlandwell.

The way curves to reach a junction. Go left here and a grassy path skirts between open fields. It curves right further on, leading to a kissing gate on the north tip of **Portmoak Moss** community woodland. There are two path options within the wood; take the left-hand one and follow it round the northern edge of the mixed plantation. There's a junction some way on; carry straight on here to join a wide path. Turn left and this leads past carved wooden benches to a gate. Go through the gate and follow the track straight on to join the public road. Turn left and follow this into **Scotlandwell**. At a junction in the centre of the village, go straight on along the **A911** following the pavement back to the start.

Bishop Hill

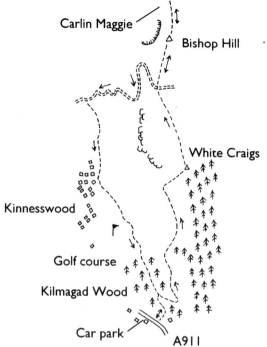

Carlin Maggie

Bishop Hill

White Craigs

Kinnesswood

Golf course

Kilmagad Wood

Car park

A911

Fact File

Distance 7.5km/4.6 miles.

Time 3 hours.

Map OS Landranger 58; OS Explorer 370.

Start Portmoak Parish Church, by Scotlandwell, grid ref NO 183019.

Parking Large free car park adjacent to church. This is available for public use except on Sundays before 11.30am when it is used by churchgoers.

How to get there Follow the M90 to junction 7, Milnathort, and then the A911 to Scotlandwell. Portmoak Parish Church is on the right, just before Scotlandwell is reached.

Terrain A moderately challenging walk through woodland and over open hillside with a strenuous section of ascent early on.

Dogs There is sheep grazing on upland sections of the route where dogs will need to be on the lead.

Facilities The Well Country Inn, Scotlandwell, does morning coffee, snacks and bar meals.

Bishop Hill offers a short but challenging hill walk where the effort is rewarded with fine views and an impressive geological landmark.

Leave the **car park**, cross the road and turn right, following the pavement towards Scotlandwell. Just beyond the Scotlandwell road sign, turn left on a path signed for Bishop Hill. The way climbs wooden steps and continues up to a stile. Cross and walk up the edge of a grassy field to another stile where there's a Woodland Trust sign for Kilmagad Hill.

Once over the stile, turn left and a good path follows a fence along the lower edge of predominantly oak and beech woodland with views west to Loch Leven. The way rises gently to a junction of paths and waymarker. Go right here and the path climbs steeply. After a concerted uphill pull through **Kilmagad Wood**, the path turns left, skirting the hillside to gain height more gently. Continue up through a small wooded area to a stile straddling a stone wall.

White Craigs is obvious ahead and there are fine views west over Loch Leven. Cross the stile and a path heads north over a flat section of hillside. Just before the slope becomes increasingly steep, the way curves right below a quarry and crosses the hillside to meet a wall and fence. The path climbs by the wall all the way to the summit of White Craigs. Bishop Hill is visible to the north, as are the summits of East and West Lomond.

A narrow path runs down the north flank of White Craigs and over grassy moor to meet and follow a track north to a point where several walls converge. Pass through the first gateway but don't follow the track, which veers north-west. Instead cross a wooden gate on the right and a path leads from here to **Bishop Hill**. There is a stone wall to be crossed before you reach the summit cairn.

From here make a short detour to view **Carlin Maggie**, a basalt column located on the escarpment. According to local lore Maggie, a witch, had an altercation here with the devil who unleashed a bolt of lightning, turning her to stone. To reach this geological marvel, walk north from the top of Bishop Hill for around 500 metres.

To continue the walk, retrace your steps over Bishop Hill and return to the track encountered before the final stretch of ascent. Once on it, turn right and head north-west to a junction. Go left here and the route descends the steep escarpment, zig-zagging as it loses height.

The track drops to a fence at the top of a field where there's a sign pointing left for 'Exit off hill via Kinnesswood'. Follow this and a narrow path heads south, skirting the top of the field before running out over open hillside. Turn right when it joins a wider grassy leading down to join the Tetley Trail above **Kinnesswood**. Bear left on the trail and follow it along above the village's **golf course** to re-enter **Kilmagad Wood** at a kissing gate. The waymarked trail leads back to the start.

The Cleish Hills

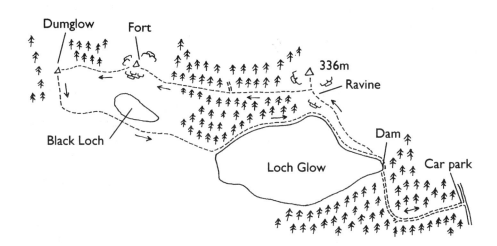

Fact File

Distance 8km/5 miles.

Time 2 hours.

Map OS Landranger 58; OS Explorer 367.

Start Forestry Commission Loch Glow car park, grid ref NT 099955.

Parking Small free car park.

How to get there Follow the M90 south to junction 5, Gairneybridge.

Leave the M90 and follow the B9097 west to Cleish Mill. Turn left and the car park is 3km south on the minor road linking Cleish Mill and Green-knowes.

Terrain Track and path throughout. Some sections can be wet underfoot. Be prepared for some short but fairly strenuous sections of ascent.

Dogs Sheep grazing on open land mean dogs will need to be on the lead for part of the walk.

Facilities None on the route.

Tucked away in the southern-most recess of Perthshire there lurks a real treat for walkers – the Cleish Hills. Overshadowed by the neighbouring Lomonds, this range of low craggy peaks dotted with small lochans and carpeted in forestry offers an excellent half day walk.

There is a small Forestry Commission **car park** just off the road at the start. Leave this at the barrier gate and head west along a good forest road. Hemmed in by trees the track reaches a junction around 500 metres on. Bear right here, remaining on the main track which descends to reach an anglers' car park at the eastern end of **Loch Glow**. Here there are fine views over the water to the various summits of the Cleish Hills.

Cross a stile by a gate ahead and follow a track skirting below the low **dam** at the head of the loch. Go over a wooden footbridge spanning the concrete outflow channel and turn left, following a fence up to a metal ladder stile. Cross and, a few metres on, leave the main lochside path and head north-west, following a fairly vague path through the grass, up the shoulder of the first 336 metre high top. The ascent is quite strenuous but good views open out over Loch Leven as height is gained. From the top of the first knoll, descend into a narrow, steep-sided **ravine** and climb on to the top of the **336 metre** high hill.

Descend back into the col and, in the base, bear right and pick up a path in the grass leading to the edge of a forestry plantation. Here an obvious path leads up through a break in the trees. There is no gate into the wood but there is a gap in the fence. The path rises through densely packed conifers, emerging on to a forest road mid-way up. Cross this and stay with the path as it disappears back into the trees.

The path exits the plantation at the top and curves right, climbing gently over grassy moor to reach the summit trig-point and cairn. An ancient **fort** once occupied this elevated spot. Pause awhile here and enjoy views east over Loch Leven and the Lomond Hills and north to the Ochils.

Leave the summit and descend west, a narrow and fairly steep path picking its way down through craggy outcrops. Cross open heather moor to reach the edge of woodland. Follow the plantation boundary west to its top corner and then head over open ground to the summit of **Dumglow**.

From here, descend south to the boundary wall. Cross it, pick up a path and go left, following the wall down to **Black Loch**. Stay with the boundary line as it crosses open ground to reach the western tip of Loch Glow. Follow a path on the northern shore round to the dam and retrace steps from here to the start.

Steele's Knowe

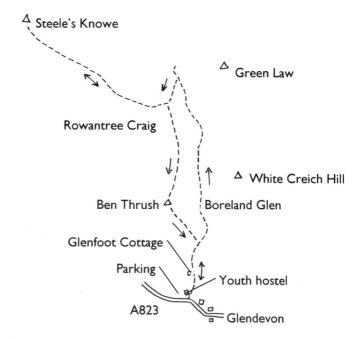

Fact File

Distance 10km/6 miles.

Time 3-4 hours.

Map OS Landranger 58; OS Explorer 366 and 369.

Start Track-end at Glendevon Youth Hostel on the A823 Auchterarder to Yetts o' Muckhart road as it enters the village of Glendevon, grid ref NN 989046. The Glendevon sign is located right next to the start.

Parking There is a tiny car park at the track end but don't block the gate or access to a neighbouring house.

How to get there Follow A9 to Gleneagles interchange, just south of Auchterarder. Leave the A9 and follow A823 south through Glen Eagles to Glendevon.

Terrain A short walk to the summit of a low hill, climbing through Borland Glen and crossing open moor. Some sections can be marshy underfoot.

Dogs There is extensive sheep grazing in Borland Glen where dogs will need to be on the leash.

Facilities None.

Steele's Knowe in the Ochil Hills offers an air of windswept remoteness. The summit is the highest point in a rolling swathe of low peaks rising to the east of Glen Eagles and to the north of Glen Devon. The ascent is relatively easy and the views from the top stretch north to the much larger mountains of the Southern Highlands.

Leave the **A823** road and, following a signed public footpath to Auchterarder, head up a track that skirts below a **youth hostel** and leads to **Glenfoot Cottage**. To the right of the house is an old metal gate with a rather faded wooden sign on it for Auchterarder. Go through the gate and follow a grassy track north across an open field. The route is marshy here and it's worth sticking to the more solid grass banks on either side of the track.

Continue towards the top left hand corner of a stone wall where the way reaches a gate and stile. Cross and head between two walls where there may be unlocked metal gates to negotiate. At the far end of this, a solid grass track leads up **Borland Glen**.

Follow the track to its highest point, on the col below **Green Law** where a gate is reached. Cross the fence here and bear left, following the fence up the grassy slope to the top of **Rowantree Craig**, where there is a tall mast. The line of the fence bears right at this point, as does the route. A grassy track heads west, following the fence over open moor.

Continue to follow the fence down into the shallow col between Rowantree Craig and Steele's Knowe. Stay with the fence for the gentle ascent of **Steele's Knowe**. Further on it is replaced by a stone dyke and, not far on, the concrete trig point marking the summit of the peak is spotted over to the right. Bear straight across the grass to reach this.

From the top of Steele's Knowe, return to the wall and follow the fence back towards the aerial mast on Rowantree Craig. Don't be tempted to take an obvious track that runs south from the trig point as it curves left down into the glen to the north of the hill.

Below the mast, cross the fence followed up from the col below Green Law and walk to the left of the wall, down into the col below and then up to a cairn marking the summit of **Ben Thrush**.

Descend east over open ground into **Borland Glen**. Stay to the left of a field below enclosed by stone walls. Take care as you descend as there is a small but steep section of crag part way down to avoid. Join the wall at the left hand end of the field and follow it down to meet the Borland Glen track taken earlier in the day. Retrace your steps to the start.

Glenearn Hills

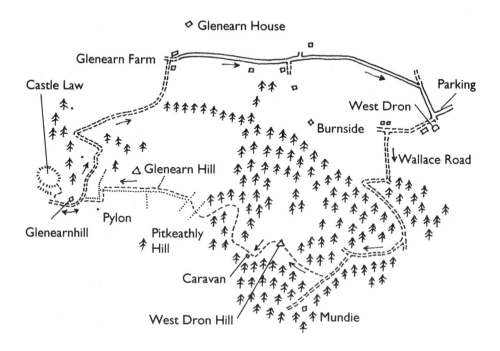

Fact File

Distance 10km/6 miles.

Time 3-4 hours.

Map OS Landranger 58; OS Explorer 369.

Start West Dron Farm, grid ref NO 126158.

Parking Road-side parking near West Dron Farm.

How to get there Follow the M90 south from Perth to junction 9, Bridge of Earn. Follow the A912 into Bridge of Earn then take first road on the left, signed for Kilgraston, Kintillo and Wicks of Baiglie. Go straight on out of town. The road passes under the M90. Take the first right to Dron, then go right. The road crosses the M90 and, 1km on, reaches West Dron.

Terrain Track and path through forestry and over open hillside.

Dogs Sheep grazing over much of the route so dogs on the lead.

Facilities Shops and pubs in Bridge of Earn.

Set off from **West Dron** down a track which heads south-west from the bend in the road. It skirts by a shed before descending to modernised cottages. Go left here, up a track signed '**Wallace Road**'. This tree-lined right of way rises gently between open fields and recently planted woodland to reach a junction.

Go right and the track passes through metal gates. It rises through a hairpin bend, skirting round the hillside to reach a fork higher up. Take the right-hand option and go through an unlocked metal gate. The track rises steadily through a wide grassy break in a coniferous forest, curving right.

Higher up a junction is reached. Go left on a grassy track which rises briefly before running level round the hillside. Continue to reach a wide firebreak which runs at right angles across the track. Go right here and a grassy path climbs on to **West Dron Hil**l. It leaves the confines of the trees and rises over an open grassy slope dotted with gorse and saplings to reach the flat grassy summit.

The route continues into the glen to the west of West Dron Hill. The western slope of the hill below the summit is guarded by a strip of trees. To avoid these descend in a south-westerly direction from the top, heading down over the slope of grass and heather to reach the wreck of a **caravan**. From here a grassy path goes right, descending to the base of the glen where it crosses the Wyllie Burn.

Continue along an obvious level grassy path, skirting round the northern flank of **Pitkeathly Hill**. Just before it emerges from the trees on to a grassy mound, go left through a firebreak in the trees. As you emerge from the conifers, bear right and head for a fence a few metres away at a stand of tall larch and oak trees.

Climb over the fence, cross the Hall Burn and head straight up the slope. Continue straight on to reach a fallen-down stone wall lined with tall beech trees. Cross this and go straight on to reach a broken-down stone wall, just beyond a small stream.

When you reach the wall, go left and follow it to reach a junction of walls. Go straight on here and a grassy track, following the wall, climbs between the two 300-metres knolls of **Glenearn Hill**. Stay with the wall and after levelling out, the way descends towards an electricity pylon line. Two pylons are visible ahead.

Just before the wall reaches another wall running at right angles, go left, heading towards the left-hand **pylon**. Immediately below the pylon another junction of walls is reached. Go right here and follow the wall down to a grassy track. Turn left and follow this to the ruins at **Glenearnhill**.

Continue up the track to a stand of larch trees where there's a stile on the right. Cross and climb up on to the summit of **Castle Law**, the site of an ancient fort and a great viewpoint.

Return to the ruins of Glenearnhill Farm and follow the track as it descends, steeply in places, to **Glenearn Farm**. Bear right on the road. Follow it back to the start.

Craig Rossie

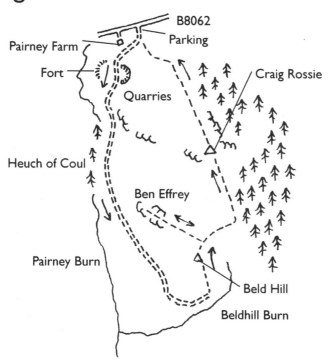

Fact File

Distance 6km/4 miles.

Time 2-3 hours.

Map OS Landranger 58; OS Explorer 368.

Start Track end at Pairney Farm, grid ref NN 978132.

Parking There are two entrances to Pairney Farm. Park at the more easterly of the two and don't block access.

How to get there Follow the A9

south from Perth then, 500 metres after it crosses the River Earn, turn left on to the B9141, signed for Dunning. Continue to Dunning then go right on the B8062 and follow this for 4.4km to reach Pairney Farm, on the left.

Terrain A well-graded ascent following tracks and rough paths, then steep descent over open hillside.

Dogs Cattle grazing around farm where dogs will need to be on the lead.

Facilities Shops, pubs and cafes in nearby Auchterarder. Bar meals also available in Aberuthven and Dunning.

Craig Rossie is a spectacular wee peak at the western end of the Ochil Hills. Rising from the fertile plains of Strathearn, the craggy summit offers excellent panoramic views.

Walk south along the track, heading away from the **B8062** road. The route curves right a short distance on and skirts behind **Pairney Farm**. It bears left, passing through disused **quarries** and below the site of an ancient **fort**. The track heads south through **Heuch of Coul**, crossing cattle grazing land where underfoot conditions can be muddy.

The way crosses Green's Burn and rises out of the base of the glen occupied by the **Pairney Burn**. It climbs over open hillside below the craggy flank of Ben Effrey. Higher up, the track curves left to meet the **Beldhill Burn**. Keep your eyes peeled for a grassy track on the left and follow this up on to the top of **Beld Hill**.

Descend north from the 365-metre high summit on a rough track and as you cross a small lump in the hillside branch left and head out on to **Ben Effrey**. The high point of this peak—at 363 metres—is a grassy mound and beyond this are the remains of an old hillfort, the steep craggy slopes below providing its former occupants with superb natural defences against enemy attack.

Return to the rough track to the north of **Beld Hill** and bear left, following it north-east up a well-graded slope to reach a fence bordering forestry. Turn left at this point and follow the fence north along the ridge, the track narrowing into a path. The way descends into a col below the southern face of **Craig Rossie**. Climb the 30 metres or so of ascent to the summit where there's a trig point and, on a clear day, extensive views.

Use the fence as a navigational aid for your descent and prepare for some steep downhill sections. The route drops north through the heather and, in places, it's easier to stray away from the fence rather than stick rigidly with it.

Continue down until you reach a corner in the fence. At this point head north-west along a path and, when it becomes vague, continue over the heather slope to reach a gate at the top corner of a field. Go through the gate and descend to reach the starting point of the route.

Abernethy Glen

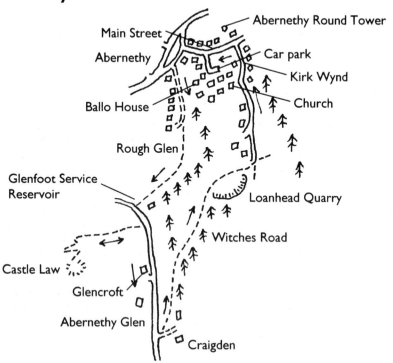

Fact File

Distance 4.6km/3 miles.

Time 1-2 hours.

Map OS Landranger 58; OS Explorer 370.

Start Inn Close public car park, Abernethy, grid ref NO 189162.

Parking Free parking.

How to get there Follow the M90 south from Perth to junction 9, Bridge of Earn, then the A912 east for 3km to Aberargie. At roundabout, take first exit on left and follow the A913 through Aberargie to Abernethy. Head into the centre of the village and the car park is signed off the Main Street.

Terrain Good track and path throughout. The optional ascent of Castle Law is short but strenuous.

Dogs Sheep grazing in fields adjacent to route means dogs will need to be under close control.

Facilities Shops, pubs and cafes in Abernethy.

This route rises through Abernethy Glen with an optional detour to the summit of Castle Law. From the **car park**, follow the access road back down to **Main Street**. Turn left and walk west along Main Street, which twists down to a road junction in front of the Corner Shop. Bear left here and the road curves right to cross Ballo Burn. On the other side, go left on a track signed 'Abernethy Glen Circular Walk'.

The way rises steadily, staying close to the burn initially. It passes the entrance to **Ballo House** and, just beyond this, a path branches left, descending to a footbridge. Don't take this but stay on the track. Higher up, the track curves right into a yard. Leave it here and carry straight on along a good path that climbs steadily between open fields. Known locally as the **Rough Glen**, this formed part of the old road from Abernethy to Strathmiglo, used to transport coal and lime.

The path emerges on to the public road at the **Glenfoot Service Reservoir**, where there is a conveniently placed wooden bench. There are good views here over the valleys of the River Earn and River Tay. Join the road and turn left. A path runs parallel with the road, leading up to the start of the Castle Law path, which is signed. To make the short detour up to this fine elevated viewpoint, follow the path. It climbs through gorse bushes, following a fence on the left.

Higher up the way zig-zags to gain height, arriving at another bench. Just beyond this, a sign for **Castle Law** points the way to the summit where there is a cairn. During the Iron Age there was a fort here, its inhabitants enjoying uninterrupted views over the surrounding countryside.

Return to the road, turn right and follow it north through **Abernethy Glen**. It rises past a house at **Glencroft**, flattens off briefly, and descends to white painted fences at the entrance to **Craigden**. Leave the road here, cross a bridge over the Ballo Burn and immediately turn left on to a path signed 'Abernethy Glen'.

The way follows the stream through deciduous woodland to reach a footbridge spanning the water. Don't cross but bear right, climbing a flight of steps. The path bears left at the top, rising to a bench by a lone Scots Pine tree.

Follow the path through woodland and above a field. This part of the route is known as the **Witches Road**. Legend has it that it was used by witches heading up Castle Law. The way skirts below disused **Loanhead Quarry** to reach a single-track road, **Kirk Wynd**. Follow this down over Tarduff Burn into Abernethy, passing the Williamson Hall and a **church** lower down. The route twists down between rows of delightful cottages to join **Main Street**.

Turn left and follow Main Street to a war memorial on the right and **Abernethy Round Tower**, which was built in the early ninth century. To complete the walk, continue along **Main Street** and, just beyond a telephone box, is the road leading up to the **car park**.

River Tay, Dunkeld

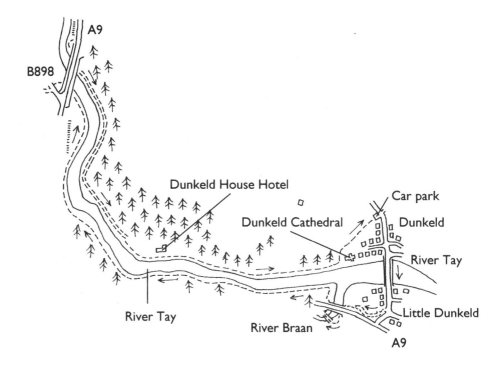

Fact File

Distance 8km/5 miles.

Time 2 hours.

Map OS Landranger 52 or 53; OS Explorer 379.

Start Public car park at the north end of Dunkeld, grid ref NO 025428.

Parking A charge is levied.

How to get there Follow the A9 north to Dunkeld. The main street leads through the town to the car park, on the left.

Terrain Low level riverside walk on well-defined footpaths.

Dogs No restrictions.

Facilities Public toilets at start. Shops, pubs and cafes in Dunkeld.

Relax by the River Tay on this delightful walk along peaceful waterside paths lined with mature deciduous trees and carpets of wildflowers. The route starts in the charming village of Dunkeld where whitewashed houses with crow-step gables and neatly clipped lawns crowd the magnificent ruins of the historic cathedral at the heart of the community. It's a popular spot for tourists, but you will quickly escape the crowds as you venture out along the riverside, sharing the calm tranquillity with the salmon fishermen.

From the **car park**, follow the main road south through **Dunkeld** and cross the bridge over the **River Tay**. Continue on, past **Little Dunkeld** on your left and, as you reach the junction with the road into Birnam, take a minor road on the right, signed for Inver. It passes a residential home and gives way to a path which skirts a sporting ground before ducking down through an underpass below the **A9**.

On the other side, cross a wooden footbridge spanning the **River Braan**, turn right and go back under the **A9**. A straight path heads off through the trees. The route meets the River Tay and curves left to follow the riverbank west. The path takes a fairly straight line through the woods, leaving the river briefly to pass a couple of ruined stone cottages before returning to the bank.

The path emerges from the trees below the towering span of a concrete viaduct taking the **A9** across the river. The path runs below this and, at a junction just beyond, turn right and go through a dark, narrow stone passage beneath a railway line. Steps lead up to the **B898**. Turn left, follow the road up to the A9 and cross the viaduct. There is a wide pavement but take care as the traffic is fast. Once over, climb over the metal crash barrier on the left and a short but steep path descends the embankment.

At the bottom, turn left and a track passes below the viaduct. It crosses an area of open grass dotted with small trees and shrubs from where a good path leads into mature woodland.

As you approach the grounds of the **Dunkeld House Hotel**, the path passes a charming little riverside stone shelter before skirting along above a strip of pebble beach popular with fishermen. Beyond the neatly trimmed front lawns of the hotel, a wide path continues, veering away from the river slightly through woodland before bearing left as it nears **Dunkeld Cathedral**.

A fenced-in path skirts round the edge of the historic site before branching left through parkland where you should bear right to return to the car park at the start.

Birnam Hill

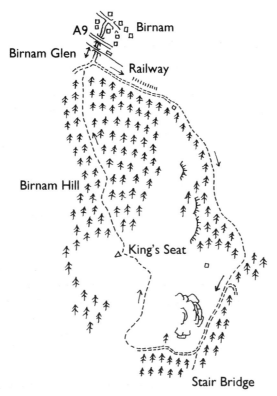

Fact File

Distance 6.4km/4 miles.

Time 2 hours.

Map OS Landranger 52 or 53; OS Explorer 379.

Start Beatrix Potter Garden, Birnam, grid ref NN 033418.

Parking Roadside layby just north of the garden.

How to get there Follow the A9 north to Birnam and the Beatrix Potter Garden is on the main street, on the left beyond the village hall.

Terrain Good paths throughout. Some fairly strenuous ascents and steep descents.

Dogs No restrictions.

Facilities Shops, pubs and café in Birnam.

A low craggy peak to the south of Dunkeld, Birnam Hill was made famous by William Shakespeare's play, Macbeth. More recently, the area attracted the author Beatrix Potter, who spent many holidays here and is said to have drawn the inspiration for some of her famous characters from the Perthshire countryside. Set off from the main street through Birnam and head up a narrow street named **Birnam Glen** to the right of the Beatrix Potter garden.

The way passes under the **A9** and, when it reaches a bridge under the **railway**, the path separates from the road and heads left at a red marker post. It climbs to houses and then a sign for Birnam Hill points left along a narrow surfaced road which soon gives way to a track running straight ahead through mixed woodland.

This leads to a private house but, as it curves right towards the property, a path breaks off to the left, descending a little over the hillside towards the railway below. It sets a course through a woodland of predominantly oak, beech and silver birch, climbing through the trees before dropping down to an open area of ground below old quarry workings on the hillside to the right.

The path meets a track from the quarry and this should be followed left down to open ground. Skirt along the edge of this and pick up a path on the right which is signed for Birnam Hill.

The way rises again and continues to do so for some distance as it climbs round the south shoulder of the hill. A strenuous pull eventually brings you up to the **Stair Bridge** viewpoint which is a short but worthwhile detour from the main route. The track continues up through the trees, curving right to level off for a short way. A flight of wooden steps and a final short climb lead to the large summit cairn on **King's Seat**. The top is a fine viewpoint with the hills to the north, including the prominent peak of Schiehallion, visible on a clear day.

Follow the path north down over open hillside. It winds through Scots pine and larch trees to reach a viewpoint overlooking Birnam and, across the River Tay, Dunkeld. The Loch of the Lowes nature reserve is visible beyond.

The way becomes steeper from here and care should be taken as you walk down through the bracken and silver birch trees to meet up with the path coming up from Birnam Glen just above the railway. Retrace your steps from here to the start.

Mill Dam and Rotmell Wood

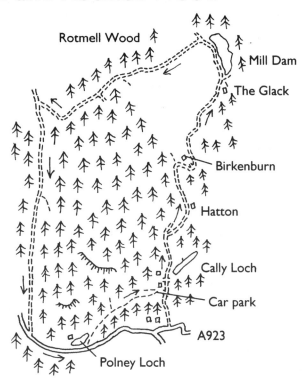

Fact File

Distance 10km/6 miles

Time 2-3 hours.

Map OS Landranger 52 or 53; OS Explorer 379.

Start Cally Car Park, Dunkeld, grid ref NO 023437.

Parking Large free car park.

How to get there Follow the A9 north to Dunkeld, then the A923 through Dunkeld, turning right on road signed for Blairgowrie. Take the second track on the left and follow this up to the car park.

Terrain Well-defined tracks and paths throughout. Some sections can be muddy underfoot.

Dogs No restrictions.

Facilities Shops, cafes and pubs in Dunkeld. There are public toilets in the public car park at the north end of the village main street.

The countryside to the north of Dunkeld is a great place for walkers and mountain-bikers. Good tracks and paths meander through tranquil woodland and over open ground, linking a string of peaceful lochans. This route offers a taste of what this scenic landscape has to offer and will hopefully inspire you to explore the area further.

Leave the **car park** and head back down the access track. When it curves right, go left on a good track passing through an open gate and heading north. At a junction by **Cally Loch**, hidden in the trees to the right, go straight on along the main track and, 400 metres on, another junction is reached. Bear right here and the route curves round the hillside to reach a cottage at **Hatton**. Carry straight on here, the track skirting between trees on the left and an open grassy field to the right where you may see fallow deer grazing.

Around 500 metres on from Hatton, the track crosses a cattle grid and enters woodland again, crossing a burn by an old stone bridge. It curves sharp right and climbs below a house at **Birkenburn**. At the top of the incline, the route turns left and, a few metres on emerges from the trees to cross open ground.

The track reaches a junction west of cottages at **The Glack**. Go straight on here, passing through a high unlocked gate. The track climbs to the southern end of **Mill Dam**, a peaceful stretch of water popular with trout fishermen.

Stay with the main track as it continues north along the west side of the lochan, passing a boatshed to reach a junction. Go left here, passing through a gate, and a grassy track rises through a gap in the hillside. It continues to climb, becoming increasingly stony underfoot, to reach the southern edge of **Rotmell Wood**, a densely packed conifer plantation.

A short way on the track enters the forest at a gate. Go straight on at a junction within the trees and, beyond this, the way descends, leaving the confines of the plantation at another gate. The track curves right and then left, dropping to a junction above the Tay Valley.

Turn left, heading south and, 500 metres on from the junction, the track enters woodland again at a high unlocked gate. A wide grassy way skirts between dense conifers on the right and an airy plantation of tall pine and larch carpeting the slopes to the left.

Stay on the main track as it gradually descends to meet the public road just beyond a gate. Turn left and walk along the wide grassy verge to **Polney Loch**. A path leaves the road and skirts along the southern bank of the lochan. Go straight on at the end of the lochan and the way rises through the trees, leading back to the car park.

Useful contacts

Perthshire Tourist Board
Lower City Mills
West Mill Street
Perth PH1 5QP

Tel: 01738 450600
Fax: 01738 444863
Web: www.perthshire.co.uk

Perth & Kinross Countryside Trust
Pullar House
35 Kinnoull Street
Perth PH1 5GD

Tel: 01738 475348
Fax: 01738 475310

Public Transport Unit
Perth & Kinross Council
Pullar House
35 Kinnoull Street
Perth PH1 5GD

Tel: 0845 3011130

Useful websites

Forestry Commission: www.forestry.gov.uk

Mountaineering Council of Scotland: www.mountaineering-scotland.org.uk

Ordnance Survey: www.ordsvy.gov.uk

Outdoors Magic: www.outdoorsmagic.com

Scottish Rights of Way & Access Society: www.scotways.com

Streetmap: www.streetmap.co.uk

VisitScotland: www.visitscotland.com

Walkscotland.com: www.walkscotland.com

Woodland Trust: www.woodland-trust.org.uk

Country Code

Guard against all risk of fire

Keep dogs under proper control

Leave all gates as you find them

Keep to paths across farmland

Avoid damaging fences, hedges and walls

Leave no litter

Safeguard water supplies

Protect wildlife, wild plants and trees

Go carefully on country roads

Respect the life of the countryside

Important note

All routes were correct at the time of publication. However, in the countryside things can change over time. For example, areas of forestry can be felled and bridges can be washed out. All of the routes in the book follow rights of way or permissive paths. However, from time to time, restrictions may be encountered, particularly in forestry during periods of felling. In such cases, be prepared to follow any diversions put in place for public safety. Remember that the countryside is a working environment for many people. Neither the author nor the publisher can accept any liability for any accident, injury or damage incurred while following any of the routes contained in this book.

Updates

If you encounter any changes or alterations to any of these routes on the ground, or experience any problems, please drop us a line and we'll investigate. Please write to Amenta Publishing, Suite 68, 17 Union Street, Dundee DD1 4BG, or email mail@amentamedia.co.uk.

Details of updates, alterations or restrictions on any of the routes will be published on the web at www.walkscotland.com/perthwalks. You'll also find a wealth of other information here, plus free access to hundreds of walks all over Scotland.

Notes

Available in the same series

Dundee Walks
BY JAMES CARRON

20 great country walks within 20 minutes drive of the city. The same format as this book
but covering the Dundee area. Includes maps, fact files and full colour cover.
Areas covered include the Sidlaw Hills, Balkello Wood, Backmuir Wood, Templeton
Forest, Clatto Reservoir, Backmuir Wood, Dronley Wood, Laird's Loch, Tullybaccart,
Kinpurney Hill, Newtyle, Crombie Country Park, Balgay Hill, Balmerino, Birkhill Wood,
Lucklaw Hill, Tentsmuir Forest and East Haven.

ISBN 0-9547028-0-8
Price: £5.00

Available from tourist information centres and book shops in the Dundee area or by
mail order from James Carron, Suite 68, 17 Union Street, Dundee DD1 4BG.
Please add £1 for postage and packing.

Cover photographs

Front cover: Binn Tower (top) and the view from the Cleish Hills (bottom). Rear
cover: Loch Glow (top) and Mill Dam (bottom). Photographs by James Carron.